Heavenly Realm Publishing
Houston, Texas

Published by, Heavenly Realm Publishing
PO Box 682532
Houston, TX 77268
1-866-216-0696

Visit our Website at: www.heavenlyrealmpublishing.com

Printed in the United States of America

ISBN—13- 978-1-937911-71-3 (soft cover)
ISBN—13- 978-1-937911-72-0 (ebook)

Library of Congress Control Number—2014907278
Stephanie Franklin
Do it On Purpose: *How to Respond When Life's Challenges Try to Pull You Away from God's Purpose for Your Life/* Stephanie Franklin

1. Self-Help : Motivational & Inspirational 2. Self-Help : Personal Growth – Success 3. Self-Help : Personal Growth – Happiness/ Stephanie Franklin

This book is printed on acid free paper.
Printed in the United States of America

Unless otherwise indicated, all scriptures quotations in this book are from the King James Version of the Holy Bible, and NIV version.

Stephanie Franklin
Stephanie Franklin Ministries
info@stephaniefranklin.org
www.stephaniefranklin.org
www.stephaniefranklinminitries.org

DO IT ON
PURPOSE

**How to Respond When Life's Challenges
Try to Pull You Away From
God's *Purpose* for Your Life**

Stephanie Franklin

For You Lord, as always.
Thank You for revealing my PURPOSE.

CONTENTS

CHAPTER ONE
Love on Purpose

CHAPTER TWO
Give on Purpose

CHAPTER THREE
Walk on Purpose

CHAPTER FOUR
Remain at Peace on Purpose

CHAPTER FIVE
A Person of Purpose

CHAPTER SIX
Do It On Purpose

DO IT ON **PURPOSE**

How to Respond When Challenges
Try to Pull You Away From
God's Purpose for Your Life

STEPHANIE FRANKLIN

Heavenly Realm Publishing
Houston, Texas

ACKNOWLEDGEMENTS

As always, I would like to thank my best friend God, my Lord and Savior. He is truly my Redeemer. I love You so much. The words in this book could not have been put together without You.

To my family and close friends, as always I love you dearly and thank you all for your support, you know who you are.

"For those who are paying the cost for purpose, just do it on purpose and watch God move. He will not fail you."

—Stephanie Franklin

PREFACE

Do It On **Purpose** is a book that opens the door for Christian Believers (young and seasoned) who have lost their way and have given up on their purpose to come back and get back on the journey. It is a book that will literally show you how and with all that is within you, to put it on purpose. Purpose is not always the easiest thing to do. In most cases, it can be very difficult and as a result, Christians across the globe have lost their way and have given up. When you have these moments, remind God of His Word. Say to Him, "It Is Written." This is how your conversation should begin with God. "Lord I'm standing on your Word. I am taking You at Your every Word and every Promise. I am putting everything I have and everything I am going through *on* **Purpose**."

Each chapter is packed with information to help you to understand your purpose, and what to do concerning your love, giving, Christian walk, peace, as a person, and what to do to remain on the purpose and the assignment that God has called and chosen you to fulfill in this life.

Do not let the foxes destroy your vine. Put all of them on your purpose and petition God to fight for you and to fulfill His promise, especially since He has assigned you to go through it anyway. I'm a strong believer that God will never assign you to do something and not give you the tools to complete it—He will do just what He said. God is your shield and your exceeding great reward *(Genesis 15:1)*.

Do It On PURPOSE

Do It On **Purpose** came to me in the mist of worship service in 2009. God spoke these words as I sat in the pews at church as I had been going through a rough time in my life and ministry. He spoke these words softly as I petitioned Him about my situation, *"Do it on purpose."* Immediately after hearing those words, my purpose dropped in my spirit. I began to think about what God had assigned me to do on this earth. The title has a great significance to it because it is talking about whatever God tells you to do, do it because it is a part of your purpose. So, whatever obstacles come your way as you follow God on the purpose that God has assigned you to do, do it on purpose, put it on purpose, put it on God. Whatever is not going right or is challenging you, do it on purpose. Through persecutions, hard trials, poverty—financial setbacks and never ending debt, recession (slumps and stagnation), bullying (someone constantly picking on you and nagging at your downfalls and mistakes), stress to progress, stress of not succeeding, just do all of them on purpose. Put them back on God to take care of the situation that is too big for you to handle.

Going through our journey of trying to fulfill what God has assigned us to do is not always easy. In fact, at times it is more challenging than it is fulfilling. It is challenging because the devil is always fighting against the work of God and His plan for his people, the young, and the seasoned. If the devil is not fighting you, you are not doing it on purpose. You are doing what the devil as assigned you to do—sin. There is a war between good and evil. Good wants to use God's people to win as many souls as it can to the Kingdom of Heaven, and evil wants to do the opposite, it wants to win as many souls as it can to hell. I have never known God to allow the devil to defeat His people. If you are going through and it seems as though God is not there, and He is not moving on your behalf, try reading this book: *"Do It On Purpose."* I guarantee you after reading it, it will answer every question, provide biblical confirmation and help, give you strength, and a new outlook on your future.

Remember, when it seems as though you cannot make it any further, just *"Do It On Purpose"* and God will give you your second wind to live and to complete your purposed life's assignment.

CHAPTER ONE

LOVE ON PURPOSE

This chapter provides a step-by-step outline on how to love on purpose. It shows you as the reader how to:

- *Love while you are in the heat of battle*
- *Love when it is not in you to love*
- *Love when you've been wounded and hurt*

Love: [noun] Warm liking or affection. Loved person. Like greatly. Loving: Feeling or showing love.

How to Love While You Are in the Heat of Battle

To love on purpose is one of the most challenging steps while fulfilling your God given purpose. I say this because when we do not love, it can be very detrimental to the other person(s) involved. It does not matter how giving you are, or how much you help and go out of your way for people, and have faith at being a part of the local church or whatever, if you do not love while doing it, it doesn't mean anything to God (*1 Corinthians*

13:2). God operates on love. His entire motive on sending His darling Son Jesus to the earth, in the flesh, was because He loved us so much that He wanted to us to believe, break the curse of death and bring eternal life. You may ask where did the curse come from? Well, the answer is located in Genesis chapter 3, when Adam and Eve disobeyed God by eating the apple from the tree of knowledge as God told them not too. At that point, the curse of sin came into the world. What was so awesome was that God already knew that Adam and Eve would disobey, so He had already planned to send his darling Son Jesus into the world to die for our sins and to break the curse from death to eternal life. This may seem too deep to you but you need to understand where all of this turmoil and torment, sickness and disease, hatred for one another, jealousy, and strife comes from. Nevertheless, the good news is the fact that Jesus came and suffered for those things that would have probably sent you and me to our graves without the chance of eternal life. God is full of mercy and grace. I believe this is why He said that His mercy endures forever *(I Chronicles16:34)*.

I'm sure while you were trying your best to love and to give God all you have as you try to fulfill His every command, the devil came in and stole your love. Right? Right. I can ask this question because it has happened to me. I was on a high, full of God's glory and love, and the devil sent someone to come against me. Immediately it threw me off and into another level. I don't care how anointed you are, or what position you hold in the church, or on your job, or how smart you are, the devil will always try to work against you to try and stop the purpose and the will of God for your life. In addition, he will also use that or those very things that you are weak at. God will fight your battles, but when you fight your battles, you are on your own. All you are required to do is speak softly and it will turn away wrath, tell the truth in love (Ephesians 4:15), and hold your course while God defeats the enemy on your behalf.

> *A soft answer turns away wrath, but grievous words stir up anger.*
>
> **Proverbs 15:1**

In your own words, write down what situation[s] you encountered that challenged your love.

_____

_____

_____

_____

_____

_____

_____

_____

_____

_____

_____

Write in your own words your response when God reminded you about His Word on how to handle a negative situation you experienced through love. If you have never encountered a negative situation, then write down how you would react if God did remind you.

_____

_____

_____

_____

_____

_____

_____

_____

_____

_____

In order to conquer the devil's plan to steal your love, you have to listen to what the Lord says to you in the mist of your battle. You are not always going to have time to go get in your prayer closet and come out with an answer or a solution to how you should react. You are going to have to deal with it right where you are and while the enemy is right in front of your face. This is why it is important once again to listen to the Holy Spirit, He will never lead you astray.

How to Love When It's Not in You to Love

We all have been raised in different situations, homes, and environments. You may have been involved in harsh and abusive situations that it has been impossible for you to love. You may have completely lost your love and refuse to listen to what the Bible says about loving others because of what people have done or said to you. I have also encountered this while ministering to some people in the past years of my ministry where they had been brutally hurt by someone or others, and have struggled to love the person(s) who hurt them or even those who were innocent and had nothing to do with what happened to them. I have also encountered a situation where the parent or guardian were not affectionate during the years of that person(s) upbringing, and as a result, when they themselves got older, they turned out the same way as the guardian or the parent. They were not responsive when their children needed to be loved, nor when the child tried to show affection toward the guardian or parent, they refused to show affection back to them. This explains why it would not be in that particular person to love.

This does not make you dumb, nor does it make you strange. It is not your fault that you were not raised to show affection or your parent(s) did not show you any affection. However, it is your fault after you have heard the truth and do not make every effort and attempt to change. I have learned just by drawing closer to the Lord that He requires us to love one another (*John*

15:12). This is a commandment. I did not realize how important this word was until I drew closer to the Lord and began to study the Bible and search out the Scriptures for truth. God began to speak to me. You are commanded to love and to forgive. This is a part of your purpose. You cannot successfully fulfill your purpose in life if you do not love because God works through love.

You may ask, "How do I show love when love is not within me?" My answer would be this, first you need to ask God to put His undying love within you. When God's love is within you, it will be easy to love when someone is trying to show you love. Also, after someone hurts you or have hurt you in the past, it will be easy to forgive them and to move on. You will not draw back from those who had nothing to do with the hurt you experienced, and you will be able to reach out and show affection toward others after experiencing the hurt you went through. Then ask God to help you to show that undying love within you. How do you show affection? What do you do to show affection? Well, here's your answer. You can simply show affection by hugging someone as you greet them. You can also show affection by saying loving and kind words to a person. For example, complimenting them on how nice their hair looks, or their outfit looks nice. You can even go and buy them a card or buy something nice for that person to show how much you love them. This is what affection means. Jesus was all of these examples and more as He completed His Kingdom assignment here on this earth. Jesus even loved His enemies. Remember Judith in the bible? He came against Jesus, and what is so amazing about Jesus is the fact that He knew Judith was not for Him—he was a hater in disguise. Ever had one? Although being His enemy, Jesus loved him anyway. In fact, Jesus loved Judith and treated him just like He never knew he was a hater. This is what God wants from His people. I realize it's hard, especially when you've been hurt so bad; and the very thought of that person brings a ball of anger to a point where you want to hurt or even to the degree of killing them. Your victory will come when you make up in your mind that you refuse to be miserable for the rest of your life. If you will notice, your enemies are gone free and enjoying their lives while you are still living in the past and mad at what happened thirty years ago. You must forgive and move on.

You must love. Loving a person can change their life forever. If you love a person, it can change a person who hurt other people to a person of love. Most of the time they hurt because they have been hurt and need love. I'm not making any excuses for their evil behavior. However, I have found that people do not hurt, or do evil for no apparent reason. There is always a reason. Whether they admit the reason or not, there is always a reason behind why they hurt you or others. This is why it is so important for every person to love and treat everybody right no matter who they are, what their culture is, color, gender, or actions.

> *Loving a person can change their life forever...*

There is a right way and a wrong way to love. The right way comes straight from 1 John 3:23. It tells us to love one another just as Jesus loves us. While growing up, my mom always told my siblings and I to love and to treat people as we want to be treated. Those words she spoke have always stuck in my mind, even when there were times I did not always do right. I too made mistakes with people, and because of my mother's words, I felt convicted afterwards and went back and apologized for my wrong. This is the love we should all have.

Now the wrong way to love would simply be not to go back and apologize even when I knew I was wrong. This is called, "pride". Pride is the number one epidemic to death in this world. There have been millions of deaths due to people refusing to say they're sorry or refusing to make amends with one another. Pride told them that they did not have to say that they were wrong even though they knew they were wrong. God's love changes what you want to do. It changes how you want to react to a situation you do not agree with. Love can add years to your life. Love changes things. Love can change anyone and anything. It changes the person, mind, body, spirit, and soul.

How to Love When You Have
Been Wounded and Hurt

Have you ever been wounded or hurt? Maybe it was by someone's words, actions or maybe even by the force of their fists. I have found that the scar from someone's words hurt worse than the force of someone actually hitting or beating on you. The force of someone's fists will eventually heal, but words can stick with you forever if you allow them to. I'm a living witness to this. My dad and I have had a rocky relationship from my teen years up until now. He lived his life through me instead of allowing me to live my own life. This caused a lot of pain for me with trying to meet his unbearable controlling expectations. The hope of his dream was to accomplish all the things that he did not accomplish in his own childhood through me. I am not making you think that my dad was a horrible person, I am only stating that he just did not allow me to be me. The more I surrendered the hurt and pain; and the closer I got to the Lord and allowed God to deliver me, the more He helped me realize that nobody is perfect. We all have hang ups and down falls, especially if you have been put in a position in your years of growing up where your parent(s) did not get the nurturing and the foundation from their parents, or from the teaching of God's Word; or from being absent in church growing up as a child. My dad did not grow up in the church so some of his actions were done not realizing that they were wrong. I now believe that he meant well, he just did not know how to handle his emotions, actions, and the way he expressed himself when he got angry. This was our biggest down fall. We would get into it constantly because I struggled with his over aggressiveness to control my life and me. If you are a dad or a mom and you are reading this book, please do not control the lives of your child or your children, or try to live your life through them. It will only cause them to reject you and to pull back from your authority. You must love them and accept them for who they are, and who they are growing up to become. Christ loves us just the way we are. He does not try to change us, nor does He make us feel bad because of our shortcomings. In addition, He does not make us feel bad when we cannot meet His expectations at times. He will convict you to change those things that you do or say that are wrong and still love you for who are you. I say this because God already knows what you are going to become, before you can see what you are going to become.

There was someone I knew who was heavily on crack cocaine, and there was a time I had to go and help him and pray for him because he was hallucinating from the drugs. At the time it appeared from the outside that he was never going to change and be delivered. He was hurt, ashamed, embarrassed, angry, and wounded and wanted to end his life. I believe that deep down on the inside he wanted to be delivered. I knew that he had faith on the inside to change, however, he was too weak to accomplish it. He was so hurt about his present marital relationship and felt like giving up, and felt like others had given up on him because of his struggle.

He did not give up and I did not give up on him. I prayed and believed God for him. I stood in the gap for his life and for the promise that God had made on his life. I took him to rehab. I knew he was purposed and called into the ministry. I loved him for who he was and he needed that. I did not throw his struggle and the fact that he had a problem in his face like some people do all over the world. I share all of this to say that as time went on, he was delivered from crack cocaine and is now a faithful minister, worship leader in a church, and is re-married to a beautiful Christian woman who loves him dearly. This is why you cannot give up on anybody. You never know what God's plan is for their life, and you never know what they are praying on the inside to God for themselves; although it may not appear on the outside that they are. You have to hang in there with them because it could be you in that same or worse position.

When you really think about it, Jesus never gives up on us. The evidence is shown by the fact that He died on the cross for each one of our sins. He took all of the pain, shame, struggles that we all have faced or are facing right now in our lives. This is a good time to say, "just *Do It On* **Purpose**... I will do it on purpose." The person I knew was purposed to become a worship leader and minister for the Gospel. God looked past his struggle, and saw his need. He saw the purpose He had for him. In prayer, I prayed for his purpose. I took God at His Word for his purpose. I put it on purpose. I put his life on his purpose—What God had sent him here on earth to do. I may not have been able to visually see it at that time, but I hung in there in prayer, and declared and decreed that God's purpose would be fulfilled in his life. I stood on the Word of God that God had to fulfill His promise and His purpose for his life. Like momma say, "when I tell you that God did it, and is still doing it, I mean just that." I am so proud of him and how he is allowing God to be first in his life, and lead the way for him. This is love. Praise God!

> *I did it on purpose. I put his life on his purpose.*

God's Word will never fail us. He says in His Word in *Joshua 23:14, "...that not one thing has failed of all the good things that the Lord your God has spoken concerning you, all have come to pass for you, and not one thing has failed."* As you read this scripture, allow it to carry you when you go through your rough and tough times, and through your most unbearable struggles. Allow it to encourage you not to give up and to give all of those things to God, totally trusting that He will not fail you—He has promised this. *Do It On Purpose.* Love *On Purpose.*

CHAPTER TWO

GIVE ON PURPOSE

This chapter provides a step by step outline on how to give on purpose. It shows you as the reader how to:

- *Give when it hurts*
- *Give out of your dry season*
- *Give when you don't have anything to give*
- *Give out of your sickness*
- *Give when everything is going good*

Give: [noun, verb] cause to have, in the abstract sense or physical sense. Give as a present; make a gift of. Dedicate; "give thought to". Render, give or supply. Establish: bring about.

How to Give When It Hurts

When you are going through, giving financially is the last thing you want to think about doing. Your mind is strictly on receiving because you have a need. When the bills are due and the electricity company is talking about turning off your lights on that same day, giving is the last thing you want to do. When all you have is $20 in the bank, and God tells you to give that entire $20 to the woman in the grocery store who is struggling with paying for her groceries, giving is the last thing you want to do. When you are in church and the Pastor has declared that that particular Sunday is the giving season for God's people to give in order to reap harvest, and all you have in the bank is $550. You just got paid and have not paid any bills which are all due, giving is the last thing on your mind. I have provided these examples because these are the number one reasons why people do not give and their faith is tested to the greatest degree.

I was once in this position and it did not feel good. I have learned, and are still learning that God will never tell you to give something and have not already have planned to give it back to you. He said in His Word in 2 Corinthians 9:6, *"...he which sow bountifully, shall reap bountifully."* This is what happens when you give when it hurts, when you give your last, and give in such a large way that it forces God and all of Heaven to act speedily on your behalf. Giving when it hurts is when God will move in such a fast way that you will not have time to turn your head. When I gave/sowed my last, the very next day God moved in miraculous way and gave me back more than what I gave the day before. The awesome thing about it is the fact that He did it in an unexpected way. Although I was expecting God to move, I was still surprised that He moved so quickly; and then the fact that

He gave me more than I asked of Him. That is how awesome and true to His Word He is.

> *I have learned, and are still learning that God will never tell you to give something and not already have planned to give it back to you.*

How to Give Out of Your Dry Season

Have you ever gave and nothing came back to you? Ever wondered if God told you to give in the first place? At times we go through a season of just sowing and not reaping. For example, there was a season that Joseph and all of Egypt sowed and gathered all of the crops that they could for seven years, and after that seven years was up, they had to reap off of what they had been told by the Lord to sow during that seven years (Genesis 41:46-47). This can also be a perfect example as to when God tells you to give and you do not see your harvest right away. This is giving out of your dry season. Be encouraged and please do not give up. It does not mean that God has every intention to forget your seed, or not to see what you have done, it is just your dry season—getting ready for your new season of harvest. Does this make sense? I sure hope so.

It is my earnest desire that God's people be blessed. I believe that it is God's earnest desire that His people be blessed. He does not want us weary in well doing and afraid to give even when nothing happens right away, or you do not see your return right away *(Galatians 6:9) (II Timothy 1:7)*. I guarantee you that He's on the way. Just keep on sowing and giving your money, time, love, faithfulness, and your effort because it will not be long before God will move for you.

> *Be encouraged and please do not give up. It does not mean that God has every intention to forget your seed, or not to see what you have done, it is just your dry season—getting ready for your season of return and harvest.*

How to Give When You Don't
Have Anything to Give

When you do not have anything to give, you give by having a giving attitude and Spirit. A giving attitude is an attitude that is positive and excited about giving, although you may not have anything financially or physically to give at that particular moment. God loves a cheerful giver *(2 Corinthians 9 :7)*. He loves it when His people are excited about giving although you're broke as a joke. The reason why He loves your excitement is because He sees the amount of faith you have and want to give. What you're telling God is, "I may not have a dime to my name, but I trust You Lord enough that if I intentionally praise You and give my last with a cheerful heart and Spirit, I know You're going to meet every need in my life, pay off every debt I owe, and put money in my bank account."

Because you are a cheerful giver, everything lines up and falls in your favor. Your family lines up, your children lines up, your enemies on your job gets out of your way and are removed, and money just falls in your hands.

How to Give out of Your Sickness

Sickness is never anything that any of us want to deal with. If we had our way, we would never be sick ever in our living lives. However, when sickness creeps up, I have found that you can sow a seed against the spirit of sickness and it must flee. I gave (sowed) a financial seed to a local church one time during a church service, and it was not long before God did just what I prayed and believed Him for. You can give a certain amount that God is leading you to give (sow), believe that He will heal you totally, and expect a return on what you gave. The key here is that you must believe, stand on His Word (spend time reading your Bible with God), and walk in faith. I can say that by God's Word you can give your way out of your sickness and watch God heal.

I am reminded of the scripture that says, *"...whatsoever a man soweth, that shall he also reap"* (Galatians 6:7). This does not always mean financially. You can give (sow) your time, love, and ability to listen to others who need a listening ear.

How to Give When Everything is Going Good

You would think giving in hard times is the hardest thing to do. However, for some, giving while everything seems to be going good is harder to do. I say this simply because, while you have the money that you have right at that moment, you want to hold on to it because you do not want to go back to where you were when you had no money at all. This is a form of fear and control. Fear and control will make you afraid to give and make you control your giving even if God led you to give. Fear will make you react this way. Fear will make you hold back while you have it for the fear of losing what you have. The best thing to do when you have money to give is to give because this is what keeps your blessings flowing. The bible says *"...it is better to give than to receive (Acts 20:35)."* This does in no way mean you give everything you have. It just means you are encouraged to give when you have it as the Holy Spirit leads you.

The more you give, the more God pours back the blessings to you. I am a living witness. The more I give, the more God gives and meet my needs. He has to honor His Word. He said if you *"sow bountifully, you shall reap bountifully" (2 Corinthians 9:6).* The abundance of blessings and favor will continue to flow in your life when you give while everything is going good. Do not wait until you do not have anything to give and wish that you could have given, when you can give now and may not ever see that day of shortage, famine, poverty, or lack in your life again. The seeds you sow while everything is going good may block the enemy's chances of robing your finances if things turn bad.

CHAPTER THREE

WALK ON PURPOSE

This chapter provides a step-by-step outline on how to walk on purpose. It shows you as the reader how to:

- *Walk after the things of God*
- *Walk into your purpose*
- *Walk when you have no legs*
- *Walk when your vision is unclear*
- *Walk when you cannot see God*

Walk: [verb] to move with your legs at a speed. To go to a place by walking. Purpose: [Noun] The reason why something is done or used: the aim or intention of something. The feeling of being determined to do or achieve something.

If you have experienced walking for a long period of time, it can be very tiring and if continued, can allow your body to have excruciating pain and even stress. There are times a Christian Believer's walk can become very tiring and very stressful when walking after God's purpose for your life. Many have given up the good fight of faith and have become very weary in well

39

doing. As a result, some have given up and have fallen from grace. I have learned in my Christian walk and purpose with God that it is a high, long, ladder to get to the divine, destined place God has purposed the Christian Believer to get to and to be. Not everyone make it there. In fact, it takes great faith and great determination to win against all odds, setbacks, and what seem like defeats. The Word of God states that faith without works is dead (James 2:20). Faith is an act of getting out there as an obedient servant and moving when God says to move, go when He says to go, and talk when He says talk. You no longer belong to you, you belong to the Lord. In the book of James, James encourages the Believer on how to be a Christian Believer. Although some Christians interpret this book as proving that good works is the cause of salvation, it is true that good works are the fruit of our good labor.

In order to please God, and do what He is calling you to do, you cannot sit and watch, make excuses when others are moving toward their purpose; or even become complacent and full of hatred for yourself and others as they go forth. You must get up and walk and keep on walking even when the walk gets tough and the road seems unbearable. No matter how long the walk may be, you cannot look at the end of the road, you must look at where you are right at that very moment, and take it one step at a time as God leads you. The Word of God teaches us to walk on purpose. Walk on what God has purposed you to be. I am going to give you several points on how to walk after your purpose:

1. Be confident of who you are and not proud or arrogant.
2. Trust God every step of the way.
3. Abide in His presence (spend time with Him daily).
4. Obey Him when He calls and gives instruction.
5. Live in harmony, love, and unity with other fellow Believers and those around you on a daily basis.

How to Walk After the Things of God

Walking after the things of God should be the most rewarding thing anyone would want to encounter. I can say that it is not always easy walking after the things of God, yet it is the most rewarding. In order to walk after the things of God, one must first have the Spirit of God (Romans 8:9). Ezekiel tells us in chapter 36:27 that God *"...will put a new spirit within you and cause you to walk in my statues, and keep my judgments, and do them."* The Holy Spirit will lead, guide, and help you to **walk** by putting His Spirit within you and by giving you the ability and help sustain you as you travel your purposed journey, no matter how long the walk may be. Nowadays, people think it is more important to make sure their family is okay and that all of their needs are met on a daily basis. However, if you are walking after the things of God, He comes first and you should make every effort to please Him first on a daily basis. As this is accomplished, your families and your needs will be taken care of on a daily basis.

Nothing and no one should take prestige over the Will of God. Your ideas or plans do not matter when following God. In fact, they are not in the running. I realize this may sound harsh, but it is the truth. God loves us all very dearly and desires to give us the desires of our heart, but fulfilling His purpose, plan, and covenant promise is more important than pleasing what you want, unless it has to do with Him getting the glory. Your wants do not matter when it comes to pleasing God's divine purpose for your life.

As you walk after the things of God, you cannot do whatever you want to do. You may not be able to go where friends and family goes at times. God may want you to get in His presence. He may want you to pray, and most times want you to pray when it is at an inconvenient time for you. I can recall a time years ago when God was first calling me to my purpose and had begun preparing me by waking my up in the early hours of the morning. It was very hard for me to wake up, let alone get in His presence. But, because God will do what He needs to do in order to accomplish what it is that He desires and needs to accomplish in you at that time, He will make sure you get what you need to accomplish it. He woke me up as if I had not fallen asleep. As He began to show me, I began to pray for individuals and circumstances of other people. I can recall His awesome presence of His Holy Spirit coming over me so strongly, which made it easier for me to pray and accomplish what He had awaken me in the first place to do. I would have never awakened on my own. God will always use us for something that brings Him glory and for somebody else's needs. I did not realize that just from my obedience and prayers that morning, the persons I was praying for were healed and got the help they needed. By obeying God and not going by what it looks like on the outside to you, may allow others to be healed, accept Jesus Christ as their Lord and Savior, and/or even change their life forever. God does not do things for no apparent reason. Although at the time you may not be able to see it, but as you obey and do it, there is always a reward in it.

> Romans 8:4 tells us *"that the righteousness of the law might be fulfilled in us who walk not after the flesh, but after the Spirit."*

How to Walk Into Your Purpose

You walk into your purpose by your obedience to do what it is that God has instructed you to do. There must be a longing to get to that place. Without this longing, you will fatigue out and become tired and very weary.

You have to learn how to paddle in the mist of every storm that may come your way and not pull the boat as if it's in your power and strength to get there your way. We all will go through storms when following God. These are called tests. Peter and the disciples went through a storm of faith where they had to trust Jesus to the fullness in order to save them. Peter made the initial contact by calling out to Jesus as Jesus bided Peter to walk on water (Matthew 14:22-33). As Jesus instructed, Peter began to walk on the water, but suddenly began to sink because his faith had weakened. We can all start out good, but as time goes on and tests, trials, disappointments or you're unsatisfied with what God has called you to do or who God has chosen you to work with come your way, you're ready to give up and throw in the towel. There were times in my Christian walk when I was disappointed by what God had instructed me to do and became very hurt and depressed. This was a set-back for me. You must stay focused even in the most excruciating and hurtful times of your life. You cannot afford to get off, then you will sink. The good news is that God is right there ready to pick you up and help you back to the boat of peace, deliverance, or whatever you need at that moment if you fall and make a mistake.

The Christian Believer must grab a hold of God's own heart. God's own heart is love. It is pure. It is kind. It is always abounding in faith and in grace. It is everything. Everything it is. I cannot imagine comparing it to any human's heart, for it is incomparable. There is no comparison to God's heart nor is He confused as to what He has chosen you to do as you are on your journey or purpose in this life. Take God at everything you own and every promise He spoke and watch Him move. *Do It On Purpose.*

Do not allow your latter, seasoned years in age keep you from fulfilling your purpose and being obedient to what God has told you to do. It is not too late.

How to Walk When You Have no Legs

There was a man from Lystra who was crippled from the time he was in his mother's womb. He had never walked before. He heard Paul speak and saw that he had faith to heal. Paul said with a loud voice, *"Stand up on your feet. And the man leaped and walked."* I share this true story in Scripture to say, **HAVE FAITH** when it seem as if you cannot go any further while on your journey. Just stick to the basics and have faith in God. The cripple man had to have enough faith to believe that he could stand up and walk. It had nothing to do with Paul having all of the faith for him, but the cripple man had to believe for himself. And, from that faith, Paul was able to agree, and their supernatural immediate faith to believe for healing was matched and healing was manifested. I share that story to say that times will get tough in your life but when your legs give out, you must believe that God will help you and will guide you in the direction that you need to go. He will never put more on you than what you can bare. If He gave you those legs, He is responsible for keeping them under you, and keeping them moving in the direction you need to go.

There is no time to get burnt out. Pick yourself up, brush yourself off, go and wash your face and hands, and get back to doing what you were doing when you had the greatest faith and motivation. Sometimes this means to go back to square one like reading a book in a quiet area, going fishing, going to an amusement park alone or with family, visiting family and friends, taking a vacation, getting a massage, get a manicure and pedicure, going to play sports at a local park, walking your dog or cat, reading your favorite motivational book that gets you going, or just doing whatever it takes to get your legs back under you again and go on.

You are not alone. You may not have a huge supporting cast. In fact, you may not have a supporting cast at all. You do not have to wait for someone to pick you up, or to pat you on the back, or to cry with you. All you need to know is that God is all you need. I know this may sound harsh but it is true. If He sees fit, He will assign (use) someone to come and give you what you need. If He has not done that, then that means He wants to be alone with you to give you what you need so that He can commune with you in order to speak to you, to comfort you, and to show you what He wants you to do. He is your legs. They belong to Him. If they fail, means either you did not keep the faith or He failed you. So make sure that you do your part and

He will do the rest. He will never fail you (Deuteronomy 31:6). You can fail you, but God will never fail you. God loves you and has great plans for your life. He means the greater good for you. His plans are not your plans, His ways are not your ways, His thoughts are not your thoughts (Isaiah 55:8). When you think He's mad at you or do not like you, trust me it is always not so. He loves you and means your good. When you think that God has turned His back on you and do not want to have anything to do with you, trust me it is always the other way around. He loves you and would never leave you nor will He ever forsake you (Hebrews 13:5). When you think He's not listening or answering when you are constantly talking and praying to Him, means He's just trying to get you to a place in Him on a regular basis where you will trust Him totally. He does not want you to allow the enemy to play tricks and deceiving games with your mind to make you think that He thinks such negative, deceiving, and evil thoughts of you. One thing to remember, you cannot do it your way. You cannot plan your life and successfully follow God. It must be His way or no way. He knows what is best.

Make today your day that you decide that you are no longer going to sit while life steadily moves forward without you. If you had these types of thoughts and anger with God, repent and get alone with Him and you will see that your legs never left you; and that He is ready to speak to you and give you what you stand in need of. He has not forgotten you. Get your motivation and determination back; and live life to its fullest with joy, love, peace, and victory in Jesus Name! Your new legs are waiting for you, rise up and walk! Thus says the Lord, *"rise up and walk and trust what I have already given to you."*

How to Walk When Your Vision is Unclear

Can you picture driving down a road in the eye of a thunderstorm and cannot see the road ahead of you, but you know you're on the right road and that is the road you must stay on to get out of the storm? There are times in your life when God will allow you to travel down a dark road where you cannot see on purpose. He will do this so that you will have to trust Him totally, and call out to Him in order to see what is up ahead to get to the next point in your life, and the vision that He has placed before you. I know this is a time of frustration for you. This is a very uncomfortable place to be in. It is a storm in your life that seems baffling and confusing. He has given the vision but it seems as though He has not given you the tools, the open doors, the favor, the direction, the Word, the encouragement that you need to get it going and to complete it. Everything you touch turns out to be nothing. Everything you invest in turns out to be a bad investment. Every loan you try to get is thrown in your face denied. Every door you open, quickly closes with someone else with your blessing. The person you told about your vision because you needed help, turns on you and does just what your vision entails. This is a hard time for you and you don't know where to go. Your road is showered with dark clouds with blinding showers of tormented rain. Debris of battles are falling and flying everywhere around you. But, you know that you are on the right road. You know that you have heard from God and you know that you are doing the right thing. You are confident that you are on the right road. This is the hardest time for you I know. I can hear you saying, "how can anybody minister encouragement to me at this time in my life? I'm too embarrassed about the debt of mess I'm in and my credit is too bad to get a loan to get me out of it. I hate that everybody can see my messed up life right now. How can you tell me that I can still fulfill my vision and purpose when I've waited too long and decades have passed? How can you tell me that I can still fulfill the vision when I'm broke half the time and making pennies on the job I'm on? How can this book tell me that everything is going to be alright when I can't see my future ahead of me? How can you tell me that I have the right vision when it is much bigger than what I can accomplish by myself? How can you tell me that the vision God has given to me is the right vision when I do not nearly have the amount of money to get it started, let alone get it going and keep it going to success? How can you tell me anything when darkness is in front of me and the success, my promise, purpose, dreams, and visions seem impossible to see? The ultimate question is how can this book help me?" My answer to you is that "it already is." I can tell you that you are in the eye of the storm and Jesus is right in front of you coaching you to keep on going. He's coaching you to step a little higher in your faith. He's saying to turn your high beams on instead of just your headlights and you will see further ahead. He's saying to turn your windshield wipers on high instead of on slow and you will that I am right in front of you guiding you every step of the way. He's saying to take your time and do not move ahead of Him. He's got the wheel. He's saying you cannot control your plans, purpose, visions, and destiny; let Him do it. He's saying get up off the couch or out of your bed so that He can help you. He's saying swallow your pride and ask for help. He's saying step out on the water and walk to Him, He is waiting for you to fully follow Him. In Matthew 14:24-33, Peter was coached by Jesus to do the same by stepping out of the boat that was being tossed back and forth by thunderstorm waves as Peter was told by Jesus to walk on the water to Him. Jesus was building Peter's faith and needed for him to totally trust Him with all that he had. God does not want you to see the end of the storm right now, all He wants you to do is to trust Him every step of the way until you get to the end.

You are in the eye of the storm and this is when things seem to get really bad before they get better. However, I guarantee you that God is with you and if you are truly following Him, He will never lead you astray (1 Kings 8:57). Many times we as

Christian Believers can lead ourselves astray by trying to fix things ourselves, and work things out our way, and think that that is the Will of God for us when it is not. I have been guilty of this myself and I had to do a self-evaluation check and realize that it was not my life. **It is the life that Jesus has placed before me to do HIS WILL and to do it HIS WAY only.**

God has given everyone a vision. Some visions may seem greater than others, while others may seem only minor. However, all visions from God are mighty. They all are great and serve their own individual, special purpose for the glorification of the Lord. They are assignments that God has instructed only that special person to do and to complete. Unfortunately, millions of Christians do not fulfill them due to,

- Lack of finances *(yet do not believe or trust that God would never give a vision without providing the wealth of channels to get it),*

- fear,*(to either step out on faith or to increase their faith after they have already made the first step),*

- slothfulness *(laziness),*

- doubt *(believe one minute when doors seem to be open and everything looks good, and doubt the next when doors shut and everything seems dim),*

- unbelief *(do not believe that God showed or gave them the vision),*

- do not care and do not take the time,

- feel they do not have the time,

- lack of confidence,

- in dysfunctional and sinful relationships that pull them from being in position to pursue and complete it,

- angry with God so they have drawn back and have given up,

- put other things before it,

- Everything is going their way and there is no need to fulfill it,

- Satisfied with their life. They have all the finances they need and feel that they can build or complete anything they want their way without God,

- Way too personal and private and do not want anybody in their personal space,

It is a good thing that God does not take us off of the face of the earth for not fulfilling His God given visions and purposes that He has given to us before we were in our mother's womb. As I stated above, many people have become complacent and really could care less. However, God is taking their visions and is giving them to those who do not mind obeying Him and doing what He has told them to do. This only serves for those who do not care and are not trying to obey God to do and to fulfill the vision. However, for those who are unclear and are trying and may be confused as to how to do it, where to go, or who to talk too, God is still with you and have given you this book to help you, and will send others to you to help you and to help push you to fulfill the vision.

Below I have provided a step-by-step plan for you to be confident on how to move toward fulfilling your purpose:

1. Repent by asking God to forgive you if you are guilty of any of the bullets listed on the previous pages.
2. Get alone with God and give yourself to constant prayer.
3. Go on a fast and stay committed until you hear from God.
4. Listen when He speaks to you and do not doubt.
5. Write the vision down on paper.
6. Pray and seek God for direction and guidance on where to go, whom to trust to share it with, and the finances to fund the vision.
7. Once you receive this Heavenly divine information, do not slow around, quickly obey, and get going on it.
8. <u>Stay</u> in constant prayer and do not tell everybody what you are doing after you have set out. As God is developing your vision, it is incomplete and if you tell everybody, they may have the potential of telling others and they may slow the process down. They cannot stop God's vision that He has for you when you are pursuing

it and trying, but they can hinder it and make you miss your season, and try to slow it down when you do not obey and keep it to yourself, unless He has shown you whom you can share it or them with.

How to Walk When You Cannot See God

In my book "Position Your Faith for Great Success," I have a chapter in titled, "Stay Close to the Vine." When you cannot see your way or you get off track and become confused on which way to go, just stay close to the Vine. What and Who is the Vine? The Vine is the Holy Spirit. Just ask the Holy Spirit to help lead and guide you to all truth and He will.

Many of us face dilemmas, setbacks, and daily frustrations of pursuing goals and do not have enough time in a day to get them accomplished. As a result, these experiences allow us to get off track and blind our eyes from seeing God. Our minds are cluttered with stress and the expectations of others while trying to please everybody. People pleasing is another word for it. With this type of turmoil, it is impossible to see God and to allow Him to lead you. Your daily activities and goals do not belong to you. In fact, when you first wake up in the morning you should ask the Holy Spirit what would He have you to do, where to go, and whom to talk too. He will guide you. I realize you may be asking, "but, what if I have a job and I can't stay at home to please the Holy Spirit?" The Holy Spirit is not the

Author of confusion (1 Corinthians 14:33). He will never tell you to do something that will cause you to lose your job. He will not ever jeopardize your safety, livelihood, or life. However, He will test you at times but His test is always set up for you to pass them, only if you follow and obey Him.

Trying to do things the wrong way can cause you not to see God. God does not cling to sin—wrong doing. As you walk this road of purpose, you must walk it the way God wants you to walk it. The Bible says that it is the road of the straight and narrow (Matthew 7:14). Although it is narrow, I believe God has provided enough room on the slim road for you to stay on it and follow Him as you enjoy your life while doing it. Do not get intimidated with this strong scripture. God meets you where you are in your life and with the faith you have. He sees that you are trying and He knows your shortcomings, failures, and struggles. He is with you coaching you every step of the way, pushing you to stay close to Him as He leads you. He is not an evil God whereas He's pushing you off the road to fail, but rather helping keep you on the road, and to stay on the road to win. He wants you win every day and in every area of your life, your family's life, and doing whatever it is that He has called you all to do. He also wants you to win in every situation you may face and in every battle that comes up against you. Go forth and win, and live victoriously, for He is with you.

CHAPTER FOUR

REMAIN AT PEACE ON PURPOSE

This chapter provides a step-by-step outline on how to remain at peace on purpose. It shows you as the reader:

- *How to remain at Peace when the devil tries to steal it*
- *How to remain at Peace when the door closes*
- *How to define the word "PEACE"*
- *How to keep your peace in the mist of your storm*

Remain: [verb] continue to exist, esp. after other similar or related people or things have ceased to exist. Purpose: [Noun] The reason why something is done or used: the aim or intention of something. The feeling of being determined to do or achieve something.

How to Remain at Peace When the Devil Tries to Steal It

Battles that come our way cannot be stopped in our lives, however, God gives us the strength and the power to remain at peace in the mist of them all. They are storms that come to make us strong. For they are the trying of our faith. They work patience in us (James 1:3). This is why we are encouraged to have joy in the mist of our tribulations (trying times, disappointments, sicknesses, confusions, and when trouble comes our way). We should rejoice in that patience works experience, and experience hope, and hope makes us not ashamed. As they work patience, He also provides a way of escape when it seems there is no way out (1 Corinthians 10:13).

Test, storms, and trials build character within you. They make who you are, and more of who God wants you to become. They help you to be strong in the face of the enemy; knowing how to shut your mouth and just let the enemy sin by him or herself. God gives you peace to maintain your composure as your flesh may want to say something back. It feels good to tell your enemies off while in the mist of them, however, there is a growing process there. How you know when God is trying to take you to another level of disciplined peace, is when you are convicted (feel bad) for your actions no matter if you are right in the situation. Conviction helps you to grow spiritually. It helps you to gain the heart of God—loving in-spite of and praying for them who spitefully mistreat you (Matthew 5:44, Luke 6:28). It does not hold grudges, anger, or unforgiveness. It is the knowing that God will take care of your enemies—vengeance is His (Romans 12:19). That is not your job, it is His and His alone. For the battle is not yours, it's the Lords (2 Chronicles 20:15).

I realize it hurts when you are faced with a difficult challenge that seems impossible to forgive and to forget. I too have been faced with challenges of hurt, anger, and disappointments that took only God to help me get through them. I would have never made it through them alone.

I suffered with the hurt of rejection for so long because of my many talents. Certain people who came across my path made it possible to reject me because they knew that God had blessed me, and had a purpose for me. They felt as if they could stop it by coming against me in every way they could. But God. He did not let them trample over me. He did not let them have their evil way with me. He protected me. God will protect you from your enemies and even in the mist of confusion, which is not even your fault. You may be facing drama that belongs to somebody else. It is not God's Will for you to be involved with someone else's drama that has nothing to do with the Will of God for your life. The outcome may <u>not</u> end up the way you think that it will if you do not make a conscious decision to follow the leading of the Lord; and make the best decision to lean toward peace that is available for you and your life. I have seen cases where a person got involved in another person's confusion and the innocent one ended up getting the worst end of the confusion. The others went away free. Run after peace for every area of your life and confusion will be hard to get in unless you allow it to.

How to Remain at Peace When the Door Closes

No one wants a door to close in his or her face, especially when you have worked so hard to open the door in the first place. How you remain at peace when the door closes in your face is to remember why the door was opened in the first place. You have to ask yourself, "was it a door that God Himself opened for me?" Or, "was it a door that I opened myself?" The door that God opens does not shut in your face. It opens other doors of supernatural beginnings, prosperity and hope, blessings beyond measure, new opportunities, new faith, new levels, more favor, and new purposes and promises: *(better home, new home, new jobs, more money in your bank account, debt free accounts, better medical coverage, happiness, peace of mind, freedom from drama—family, friends, relationship, etc.).*

So, when a door closes in your face and it is a door that God has opened, it is not closed in your face, God is saying "I'm done with what was behind that door, now it is time to move to the next door." You cannot become complacent and comfortable. God is always moving and using His people in ways that will bring change and opportunity for His glory all over the world. There is much territory to travel and millions of lives still to change and heal. This is why you cannot become complacent. He does not want His people to become used to the old way of doing things and those old people who is always in your circle. Some should be there and some should not. There is more for you and that particular door that seemed to have closed in your face is merely an open door to your next level. So, I say to you, this should give you the peace you need to know that God has your back and He is on the way to give you everything you need.

What changes things are when you yourself have opened a door that God did not open. This brings confusion, miss interpretation, and misunderstanding. Doors that God do not open are doors that are temporary, and they are vulnerable for satan's attacks at any time. The door that God opens is safe at all times. You can count on that. You can never lose when it is an open door from God. Trust God in your journey in life and make sure you give yourself to prayer and supplication when trying to decide what door to take or to walk through. God will give you a peace and a knowing within when it is a door from Him. It is the Holy Spirit's job to make sure you choose the right door because He promises never to lead you astray. He will make sure you go through the right one for His purpose.

When God is leading your purpose, it is never about you, it is always about someone else. He has a plan for that other person and He wants to use you to get them there. There is mentorship in this. I'm sure you are saying, "What about me?" Well, I say the same thing about you. He will use someone to help you. You will get what you need as well. There is no need to be selfish. Just make sure you are in the right place with God and not in a place where you will suffer the consequences of missing God, because you chose a door on your own and are in a place that He have not led you.

How to Define the Word "Peace"

1. Peace is knowing who you are in the mist of adversity.
2. Peace is the supernatural trust in God when you do not hear His voice of instruction.
3. Peace is trusting God even when you cannot see your next step.
4. Peace is trust no matter what—when the fork is before you and you do not know which way to go, or the right decisions to make (finances, bills, relationships, right church, etc.), you must trust no matter what.
5. Peace is having confidence in yourself when you do not believe it yourself.
6. Peace is removing yourself from disturbances, war, and violence from within and around you.
7. Peace is shutting yourself alone with God for His perfect peace—rest, silence from a noisy situation (home, husband, wife, children, family, friends, television, phone, demanding job, etc.).
8. Peace is serenity. It is tranquility. It is calmness when your world seems to be tumbling down.

9. Peace does not focus on the absence of trouble, but it focuses on God's promise of perfect peace that He freely gives (Isaiah 26:3).

10. Peace is what everybody wants and so few have it.

11. Peace is what everybody needs but some do not want it.

12. Peace is the ability to smile when you want to cry.

13. Peace is the ability to obtain peace in the mist of adversity.

14. Peace is the ability to remain at peace while your enemies are before you.

Although I have given several examples on peace, there are many more definitions and opinions on what peace could mean to you. You can only determine what peace really means to you when you really needed it.

No one knows you like you do. No one knows your life like you do. No one knows what you go through on a daily basis like you do. This is why you can only define peace for your situation and grab a hold of God's love and concern He has for everyone who needs peace. He says in Isaiah 26:3 that *"He will keep you in perfect peace whose mind is stayed on Him."* That passage of scripture ends by saying, *"because he* (you) *trust in Him."* You have to trust God and keep your mind completely focused on Him in order to receive and maintain peace. You can never receive peace by yelling back at those who make you upset, throwing smart remarks at you, or picking at your areas of weakness. It is the job of the devil to send darts at you as he uses those around you to do it. Most times, it is those closes to you. As they hurt you, it hurts worse than it would if it were someone you do not know. However, if you do what the Scripture states, to "keep your mind stayed on Him" and trust Him every day for your peace, you will win and gain victory as you go on your day-to-day journey in this life (Isaiah 26:3).

Peace is not an easy thing to maintain, it is a challenge for most people. It is almost impossible for some to hold on to, or better yet, to grab a hold of while in the mist of daily challenges and unexpected difficult battles. Some do not want it because it makes them feel weak or inferior to those who may come off stronger than them. I can tell you when you obtain peace in your life, it will not only make you a winner in the end, but it will keep you from sicknesses like heart attacks, stokes, and nervous breakdowns. God will never put more on you than what you can bear. In fact, He will always make a way of escape for you and if you allow the Holy Spirit to speak to you, He will lead and guide you out of the battle that was set before you as a trap to steal your peace. God always win. He may not be winning in some areas in your life where you think He should, but He is still yet faithful and is able to give you peace as you are waiting for Him to move. He will give you peace and grace to maintain and not to give up. This is my definition of peace.

How to Keep Your Peace in the Mist of Your Storm

As I have spoken about storms earlier in this chapter, I want to give a greater example of how to keep your peace in the mist of your storms. As I have said before, storms come to make you a stronger person. They come to build character in you. They come for a purpose and they do come. No one can stop a storm from coming in your life. Some come great and some come small. Some come fast, and some come slow; and seem is if they will never leave. Storms make you either give up or turn to God for help. Giving up is not an option if you are reading this book. I will never encourage you to give up. There have been storms in my life when giving up was a first option. However, God's grace was sufficient for me and it allowed me to re-think the consequences, the setbacks, and all of the people it would hurt if I did. It would not only hurt me, but I would hurt others.

I have found out that others were tied to me and to my purpose in life. I never knew how much of an important role I had before being in that position of wanting to give up. You may not realize it, but you two have an important role in your life. You may not be a popular person who is well known all over the world or even locally, but you are still a role model for those who are important around you. For example, if you are a mother or father, you are a role model for your children, and they look up to you, love, and need you dearly. They may not show it everyday, but they do. If you are a husband or a wife, your spouse holds you in high regard; and look up to you and love you dearly. They need you as you need them. If you are a teenager or young adult, your mother and father or person who takes care of you loves and cares for you. So, giving up is not an option. Allow peace to be your guide in the mist of your storms, it will make it much easier for you to conquer and be victorious, while coming out without any damages and setbacks. *Do It On Purpose.*

CHAPTER FIVE

A PERSON OF PURPOSE

This chapter provides a step-by-step outline on how to remain a person of purpose. It shows you as the reader how to:

- *How to become a person of purpose*
- *How to stay a person of purpose*
- *How to act like a person of purpose*
- *How to know prayer is the key to being the person of purpose*

Purpose: [Noun] The reason why something is done or used: the aim or intention of something. The feeling of being determined to do or achieve something. The reason for which something is done or created or for which something exists.

How to Become a Person of Purpose

Becoming a person of purpose is often quite challenging especially when you do not know your purpose in life. It is easy for someone who is purposed to be a writer, they know all they have to do is to find out what to write about and write it.

However, for a person who is lost and the word "purpose" is greek to them, this can be an uncomfortable place and position.

Being a person of purpose is to totally dedicate and devote yourself and your life after the things of God. As you dedicate and devote your life after the things of God, He will show you exactly what you were sent to this earth to do. The greatest example that I can give you is Jesus. He is the greatest example to use for purpose. God had a mission before coming to earth in the form of Himself—Jesus Christ as man in His own image—God. His purpose was to come and to save His people from their sins by dying on the cross and by raising Himself from the dead, which is proven by His precious Holy Spirit that lives within those who belong to Him. This was Jesus' purpose and He knew His purpose. He was confident in His purpose, although He did not want to do it, He knew that it had to be done; and that it was not His Will but the Will of the Father (Matthew 26:39).

Your purpose is just like Jesus. It may not be as mighty and as supernatural as to save the entire world from their sins, but it is to make a Godly impact on the lives of others. The Word of God states that many are called, but few are chosen (Matthew 22:14). You were chosen and bought with a price. Jesus paid a price for you to walk in His image, pursue your purpose for His glory, and to make an impact on the lives of other believers and unbelievers. As I mentioned in my book, "Position Your Faith for Great Success," do not allow this area in your life to overwhelm you, take one day at a time as you seek the direction of God through prayer and His purpose for your life. I guarantee you it will not take Him long because He is always ready for His people to do His divine Will and purpose. Make sure that, as you are in prayer that you keep your eyes open for the prophetic Word He gives to you. You may not hear Him say it, He may use someone to come and tell you, or He may use an open door. Do you remember this in the last chapter? That is funny but it is true. It may not come in some supernatural way as to hear an audible voice from Heaven speak in your ears and say, "I have come to give you your purpose." However, it may come by anybody and anything. He will come in any way He can in order to help you to believe and know what to do. He meets you where you are. I'm not sure if you ever heard of this saying, God will take fools to conform the wise. God will take what the world thinks is foolish to make an example that He does not need humans to bring about, to perfect, and to accomplish what He wants to do in your life.

God helped me go on in times of adversity. God has helped me run to my purpose. God may send you someone who will be there for and with you to push you toward the things that He has gifted you to do. He may send you a situation where a perfect stranger will speak to you and tell you what you should be doing and you never see them again. Most times your purpose is the gifts that God has given to you for the edification of His use.

Below I have given various examples of your gifts that can serve as your purpose:

1. A gift to pray. Your purpose is most likely a prayer warrior who prays and missionizes the city and world, bringing those who are lost to believe in Jesus Christ.

2. A gift to love. Your purpose is most likely to love others who have been wounded and hurt, and to help them to see that God is love and He loves them.

3. A gift to prophesy things from God. Your purpose is most likely to be God's messenger to prophesy truth to those who need to hear the truth and direction from Him for their lives.

4. A gift to help. Your purpose is mostly to help others in areas they need help in. Trust me, most people do not have this gift. They seek to please themselves and not others, although we all should be ready and willing to lend a helping hand where ever is needed.

5. A gift to sing. Your purpose is most likely to sing for God's glory. There are all sorts of avenues for this gift. You can use this gift in the kitchen at home, use it at church for praise and worship, you can use it to record a CD or DVD. These gifts will always be to God's glory and not yours this is why He gave it to you in the first place.

Okay, I know you are saying these are much more spiritual than what I need; I need something more practical to my everyday life. Well, here they are. I am going to give you some practical examples of knowing your purpose for God's edification and use.

1. Having a gift to sew and make clothing. Your purpose is most likely to make clothes for those who may not have any and no money to get them. God may lead you to open up a shelter and give to those who are in need, or your own boutique using your own clothing.

2. Having a gift to administrate. Your purpose is most likely to lead and to oversee a large group of people at once, as God may lead you to a job where you will lead others and mentor them and teach them.

3. Having a gift to teach. Your purpose most likely is to teach others (children, youth, or adults) positive things and the righteous way to live. You do not always have to teach in a Christian setting with this type of gift, but wherever you use this teaching gift, you should always speak positive as with the information and assignment you have been given. God will open doors for His Glory.

God gives purposes for His glory and gain. It is never for our gain. Even in the secular world—on your job, at a grocery store, at a nail and beauty shop, at the mechanic shop getting your vehicle fixed, etc. So, I know you may say "if I sew clothing for those who are in need, I won't make any money to take care of myself and my family." Well, I will beg to differ there. God is the One who will supply all of your needs. He will always make sure that you have what you need and that you do not get kicked out on the street. However, do not allow your mind to focus on you. It should always be on how to make a difference in the lives of others. The more you remove self out of the way, the more your needs and desires will take affect and come to a reality. You will be happy and you do not have to worry about being left out. That is not God's nature to use you and then leave you out. It is always His desire to take care of you and supply your needs (Philippians 4:19). He knows them before you even ask Him (Matthew 6:8). The only hindrance is, is when you doubt and ask amiss (James 4:3). You do not believe or have faith and confidence that He can use a person like you. You were created to be used by God or else He would not have created you. You were not created to sit down and do nothing. God has a plan for you and His plan is always for your good and never for your bad, or something negative and detrimental to your health and life. That is not God's nature. He created love and purpose. He died for love and purpose. All you have to do is keep your mind on what He is leading you to do, no matter what your age is, and the rest is history. *Do It On* **Purpose.**

How to Stay a Person of Purpose

Once you find what your purpose is, you can from there seek God on how to perfect your purpose. How can you better the area in which you were called to do? You do not have to ask God to perfect this area. He is always, if you are abiding in Him, is always perfecting this area so that you can grow as you operate in your purpose and calling. I have listed below some points for you on how to stay a person of purpose:

1. By constantly operating in the anointing and the gifts that God has given to you.
2. By staying in your lane and not in others. The key is to keep your mind on your own vision and purpose as you look straight ahead and not to the left or right.
3. Do not get side tracked. Stay away from distractions. Distractions are people or things that will keep you from fulfilling your purpose.
4. Keep yourself to prayer on a daily basis. Prayer is needed if you want to remain focused.
5. Jot down your goals on paper and strive to fulfill each one of them one by one daily. If you're really good, you can fulfill more than one of your goals at one time.
6. Go to workshops and conferences that can help you perfect your purpose.

You are anointed to do what God has purposed you to do. For example, David was purposed to beat the big giant Goliath rather than his brothers who appeared to be the bigger, stronger, and the chosen ones. David proved that God does not go by what we look like on the outside, He goes by the heart and by your faith. David was chosen and divinely purposed to be King. God had already anointed him for this purpose, time, and tedious service. No one could do it but him. Moses is another one. No one else could have ever led the people of Israel out of Egypt and across the Red the Sea as the deep sea waters miraculously parted before them leading them to safety (Exodus 14:21-31).

You were handpicked by God, pointed out and purposed to do a particular work. The purpose may be a hard one for you but God will give you the strength and the wisdom to complete the task that is before you. He knows how much He can put on you and it will always be rewarding and to His glory. It may not be something great, but it will serve the same in God's eyes. So do not size your purpose up with others just because your purpose and calling does not seem as mighty or great or big or large. It does not mean that it is less important and worthless. All purposes are great, big, large, and mighty to God.

Do not allow the enemy to plant seeds of confusion and jealousy in your heart towards others who have a greater purpose and work than you do. Their purpose is no more greater than yours. We are all anointed for what God has chosen. And with that said, stay in your place as you do not look at what others who are called and purposed are doing, but focus on your purpose and complete it to the best of your ability and faith as God leads you. Too many times we get off track and this will get you off of your ladder of purpose and on someone else's. This is not the Will of God for you. Stay on what He has called you to do and nothing and no one else's. This can cause His anointing to lift and keep you bound. This will cause you not to be able to function because you are out of order, out of position, and off of your own purpose. As you remain on your purpose, this is staying a person of purpose.

Purposes are always linked together. We are the Body of Believers in this world to come together and work our purposes together. God created us to work together. You can guarantee what He has given to you to do, will always work with someone else or team up with them to complete the task. This forms a community of Believers to draw together, believe together, pray together, cry together, work the tedious and stressful task together that is placed before you. You are covenanted together for such a time as this. For example, Nehemiah and the rebuilding of the Jerusalem wall. It obviously took more than one to complete the task of rebuilding the great wall. The Bible says they all came together and had a mind to work as they all came together to finish the building of the wall at Nehemiah's instructions. They had to face adversity and attacks from their

75

enemies. But they all came together, prayed together, and believed together; and the Lord blessed. They were considered as a Community of Believers. Who were purposed to come together with one mind and Spirit to accomplish the task that God had called and chosen each one of them to do. They all had different assignments to fulfill as they each stayed in their places and focused on what their positions entailed. As a result, the wall was built (Nehemiah 3, 4).

It is very difficult to do what you were purposed to do if you are not abiding in God. There is great struggle. God is the only One Who leads you as you seek and do His purpose for your life. However, there is no way it can be completed if you are not abiding in Him and with Him:

1. Praying
2. Seeking him for constant direction
3. Fasting
4. Being obedient
5. Spending time in His Word.

Abide in Him and stay on the Vine and do not get off. The Vine is the Lord and there are all kinds of nourishments and fulfillments when you are on the Vine. When you get lonely and depressed, stay on the Vine and it will comfort you and bring you peace when it seems as if God is not there to give you instruction on what to do and where to go.

Moses knows how you feel. He two got confused as he led the people of Israel up to the red sea and it appeared that the Egyptian soldiers were going to consume them. But as Moses quickly inquired of God, His Word quickly came with the breakthrough of the rod. You may be in this position where you have been obedient and you have listened to God as you are doing your purpose. But now, you are at a standstill and the next step seems impossible. You don't know who to talk to and you don't know where to go. It seems as if God has left you and you are at a crossroads. I say, be patient and rest and wait on the Lord. If He have not spoken to you, it means that He is not ready for you to make the next step. It is for you to rest and seek Him and He will then give you instruction. Many times as we are pursuing our purpose, we get in a hurry, or we pursue our own purpose and not God's purpose. Let your purpose be God's as you let God be God. Your purpose is not going anywhere. It is waiting on you because you are the only one that God has picked to do it. Moreover, you do not have to worry if someone is going to take your place and leave you out. Impossible! The Bible says, "be anxious for nothing... (Philippians 4:6-8)." Do not be in such a hurry that you miss God rather than if you rest, seek, and wait on God, you'll be right where you need to be—in your place of purpose. Nehemiah can tell you this as he accomplished this so well. I challenge you to read the book of Nehemiah. It has so many revelations in it that you may need.

You may have read it before, but I encourage you to read it again. God is always speaking. You may get something new from Him.

How to Act Like a Person of Purpose

Be yourself in acting like a person of purpose. When I say be yourself, I have to be careful in saying that because being yourself requires walking in the integrity and attitude of God. It is not acting in a way that is unseemly and drawing negative attention to yourself and others. It is not making a mockery of yourself and important people around you. It is being bold in who you are, knowing who you, and Who you belong too. It is following the things and ways of God. It is thinking like God. You are not out of control with discipline. Always remember that you are representing God and His Kingdom. He is counting on you to make a positive and glorious impression, one that when you leave the scene of the unbeliever or those who you are sent to help and to do a work, they will not be left wondering if you were a child of God.

How to Know Prayer is the Key to Being the Person of Purpose

Prayer is always the key to being the person of purpose. In fact, prayer is the key for everything. It is the channel to God. It is the access that unlocks the door that we need to communicate with God. Prayer is a two way street, not a one way street. It must be a sweet communion between <u>you</u> and <u>the Father</u> as you speak to Him and He speaks to you. There is a connection and from there, every problem, question, or answer you need is given to you. Moses was perfect with this sweet communion as he went on the mountaintop to commune with God for forty days and for forty nights. As a result, as God spoke, he knew his purpose was to write the Ten Commandments (Exodus 34:28). He would not have known that had he not spent time with God and communed with God. This is how you know that prayer is the key. You receive your divine assignment, it is completed, positive outcomes are the result, and no one is left unhappy—people are helped, people are changed, people are healed, people are delivered, and people are united and not torn apart. God's glory wins.

CHAPTER SIX

DO IT ON PURPOSE

This chapter provides a step-by-step outline on how to do it on purpose. It shows you as the reader:

- *God's Purpose, Man's Promise (Gen. 50:18-23)*
- *Do it On Purpose*
- *It is Written*

Purpose: [Noun] The reason why something is done or used: the aim or intention of something. The feeling of being determined to do or achieve something. The reason for which something is done or created or for which something exists.

God's Purpose, Man's Promise (Gen. 50:18-23). Everything you do should be done on purpose. Meaning, you do it for the purpose that God has chosen you to do. It is God's Purpose and your promise (Genesis 50:18-23). You may be going through, or have gone through many dark days, suffered persecutions, sicknesses, and punishments you did not deserve for the Lord's sake just as Joseph did. His encouraging words allows us to know in verse 19-20, that now he is "in a place of God," where he now understands and recognizes that it was God Who allowed him to go through what he went through for his purpose. In order to get Joseph in a place in God, He had to set him up to be used for such a time as that—to save his father, family, and brothers who were at one time his adversaries out of poverty. He also allows us know that we may not always understand why God chooses us to go through much hardship and pain for the sake of the gospel, but know that He is setting you up for the promise that is temporarily stored up inside of you. It is not time for you to give birth yet, for the promise is not yet ready. Joseph had to be thrown in the hole, sold into slavery, falsely accused, spent time in prison, and finally and immediately were promoted; which was the birthing of his promise. It was not yet time because God had to work a work in Joseph, prepare him, and put him in position. God has to work a work in us in order to prepare us so that when we get to the place of promise He is preparing, we are humble, strong, wise, and ready to receive the promise. Joseph's purpose and promise was to save his family, especially his father from poverty. God used Joseph for His glory and brought his brothers back to apologize, and as a result, the devil did not get the glory in all of their lives, the Lord did.

God will always shine in the process. You do not shine, only God. Although God allows you to be honored by others for how obedient you were in allowing Him to use you to do such a work. But, His Name should always shine on top. A great person to use would be Mordecai in the book of Esther. He loved and honored God insomuch that he would not bow to man (Haman) (Esther 3:2). He was hated and punished for this. But God remembered Mordecai by the king and what he had done. He turned the punishment his enemies had against him against themselves, and made the reward his enemies had set up for him turn around against themselves. To Mordecai's reward, his enemies got their due punishment. They did not win and gave an account for all of their evil (Esther, chapter 6-10) (Read the entire book is encouraged). As a result, Mordecai was honored and rewarded before all the people. God will remember you when you stand for Him. He will remember the pain, hardship, and the persecution you took for Him. He will remember you when you are faithful and do not turn against Him. He will let you shine for the good deeds and love you have shown to others. This is God's purpose and Man's promise.

Do it On Purpose

Everything you do, do it on purpose. When trials and difficulties come your way, do it on purpose. Put them back on God. Take Him at His every Word and promise. When it seems as if God is not there and have stuck you in a foreign place, do it on purpose. Keep a positive attitude as you do it on purpose. Stay close to God as you do it on purpose. Keep your trust in God as you do it on purpose. Everyday may not be a day where the fruits of God are within you, but this is the time you have to suck it up and do not look at what is before you, but look at the promise of what has been shown to you by God. When I went through unbearable and unchanging challenges in the past, I would always say, "it can't last always." This I say to you to, "it can't last always." God is with you to give you an expected end, and not a dead end just as He did for Joseph.

It is Written

As you do it on purpose, constantly stand on the Word of God. Say, "it is written in the Word of God." God honors His Word. He cannot lie nor can He reverse His promise (Numbers 23:19-20). His Word will not return back to Him void (Isaiah 55:11). But it will accomplish that which it has been sent out to accomplish, and will not return back to Him void. And, if it will not return back to Him void, certainly it will not return back to you void. *Do It On* **Purpose.**

SCRIPTURAL REFERENCES

Preface
Genesis 15:1

Chapter One

1 Corinthians 13:2
Genesis 3
1 Corinthians 16:34
Proverbs 15:1

John 15:12
John 3:23
Joshua 23:14

Chapter Two

Galatians 6:9
2 Timothy 1:7
2 Corinthians 9:7

Galatians 6:7
Acts 20:35
2 Corinthians 9:7

Chapter Three

James 2:20
Romans 8:9
Ezekiel 36:27
Deuteronomy 31:6

Isaiah 55:8
Hebrews 13:5
Matthew 14:24-32

Chapter Four

James 1:3
1 Corinthians 10:13
Matthew 5:44

Luke 6:28
Romans 12:19
2 Corinthians 20:15

Chapter Five

Matthew 22:14

Philippians 4:19

Matthew 6:8
James 4:3
Exodus 14:21-31

Philippians 4:6-8
Nehemiah 3, 4
Exodus 34:28

Chapter Six
Genesis 50:18-23
Esther 6-10

Numbers 23:19-20
Isaiah 55:11

OTHER BOOKS BY STEPHANIE

1. When Ramona Got Her Groove Back from God
2. My Song of Solomon
3. My Song of Solomon *Prayer Journal*
4. Position Your Faith for Great Success
5. Position Your Faith for Great Success *Workbook*
6. The Purpose Chaser: *For Children Ages 5 to 12*
7. God Loves *Thugs* Too!
8. The Locker Room Experience: *For the Struggling Athlete & Coach, & Tips on How to Get Recruited in Sports*
9. Church Hurt: *How to Heal & Overcome It*
10. Do it On Purpose: *How to Respond When Life's Challenges Try to Pull You Away from God's Purpose for Your Life*
11. The Power of Healing
12. The Power of the Holy Spirit
13. REshape YOU: *A Fitness Guide to Teach You How to Create the New You From the Inside Out*
14. REshape YOU Elderly Fitness Exercises and Eating Plan Book: *A Fitness Book of Simple Exercises & Eating Plans for the Elderly*

CONTACT

For bookings for booksignings, speaking engagements, ordering books, etc.:

STEPHANIE FRANKLIN
STEPHANIE FRANKLIN MINISTRIES
PO BOX 682532
HOUSTON, TX 77268

EMAIL:
info@stephaniefranklin.org

WEBSITE:
www.stephaniefranklin.org
www.stephaniefranklinministries.org

Stephanie Franklin, M.A. (T.S.), MDIV

Obtains a Master of Arts degree in Theological Studies and a
Master of Divinity, and has a vision to reach the world with
her mentoring, teaching, life coaching, and prophetic preach
ministry. She has a heart to reach the youth and young adults
along with the entire family, bringing them all together as a
unified fold. One of her greatest desires is to be used by God
in whatever capacity He chooses.

www.ingramcontent.com/pod-product-compliance
Lightning Source LLC
Chambersburg PA
CBHW071744090426
42738CB00011B/2565